# Adventures
## of
# Rose and Auden

ISBN 979-8-89345-385-0 (paperback)
ISBN 979-8-89130-537-3 (hardcover)
ISBN 979-8-89130-538-0 (digital)



Christian Faith Publishing
832 Park Avenue
Meadville, PA 16335
www.christianfaithpublishing.com

Printed in the United States of America

# Adventures of Rose and Auden

Kayla Walker

Hi. My name is Rose, like the flower with thorns, because I'm beautiful and tough.

I love exploring and adventuring. I also love experimenting and problem-solving. Come along with me for a totally awesome adventure.

But first, you must meet my very best friend, Auden. She is so funny and smart, and I know you will love her too. She has special needs. All that means is she expresses herself differently. She is unable to speak clearly, but we are such good friends that I know exactly what she is saying.

When I grow up, I want to be a speech-language pathologist so I can help others like Auden.

We do everything together, like riding on her side by side. We shout to her dad to drive faster over the hills and around the curves, laughing and giggling while the wind blows our hair.

We love going undie, aka swimming. We splash around, knock each other off the floats, and jump off the diving board.

We play basketball. Auden is really good at defense, and I can hit layups with either hand! We dream of being in the WNBA.

WNBA
08
01

Eating is also a hobby of ours. I mean, these adventures do bring on a big appetite. We feast on hot dogs, tacos, pizza, and happy cake (birthday cake), and occasionally, we get a special dinner at our favorite restaurant: Outback Steakhouse.

On Sundays we always go to church. We get to worship, sing, and praise Jesus. After all, He has done so much for us, like blessing me with Auden as a friend.

For today's adventure, we are going to the river. We live in the Appalachian Mountains, so on a hot day like today, a cool mountain river will be fun to explore.

We scope out the best spots to play in. We scan the river until we find the perfect private island!

To get there, we must swim across the swift current. We hop
in a little up stream and swim as fast as we can to get to the island.
Auden beats me there. She's an excellent swimmer.

We get to work claiming our island. We make a flag out of a stick and some leaves. We decorate by rubbing two wet rocks together to make paint. We find the biggest boulders on the island to paint pictures on with our homemade paint.

PAINT
PAINT
PAINT

We throw rocks in the water as cannonballs to keep away any pirates. We use the river's current to create the best slide ever! We explore the bottom of the river and find a few fish and a turtle!

The day can't get any better, but our parents call for us to go back home. They do surprise us with a stop for ice cream, which is the best ending for a perfect day.

Until our next adventure!

# About the Author

**K**ayla is a Christian girl who loves showing God's grace to others. She grew up in East Tennessee and is a graduate of Maryville College. Growing up in the Smoky Mountains, she loves hiking and exploring the natural beauty God provided. Through writing, she hopes to teach kids they can be friends with those who are different and show there is no need to act differently.